AF615104

SOCIAL WELFARE

A FIRST BOOK
FRANKLIN WATTS | NEW YORK | LONDON | 1976

SOCIAL WELFARE

BY WALTER DEAN MYERS

Library of Congress Cataloging in Publication Data

Myers, Walter Dean, 1937–
Social welfare.

(A First book)
Includes index.
SUMMARY: An explanation of the current assistance system for the poor in the United States and some alternative programs to consider for the future.
1. Public welfare — United States — Juvenile literature. [1. Public welfare] I. Title.
HV91.M94 361.6′2′0973 76–16552
ISBN 0-531-00340-X

Photographs courtesy of: The Jacob A. Riis Collection, Museum of the City of New York: pp. 2, 5; The Bettmann Archive, p. 6; Wide World Photos: p. 8; Library of Congress: p. 12; United Press International: pp. 15, 38, 56; U.S. Department of Agriculture: photo by Jack Schneider, p. 18, U.S.D.A. Food and Nutrition Service: pp. 24, 34; New York City Agency for Child Development: p. 23; ACTION: p. 27; New York State Urban Development Corporation: p. 37, photo by Bill Rothschild: p. 28; U.S. Department of Housing and Urban Development: p. 36; State of New York Department of Labor: p. 43.

Cover design by Frances Jetter

Printed in the United States of America
6 5 4 3 2 1

CONTENTS

THE POOR IN AMERICA

Human beings have four basic needs — food, shelter, clothing, and medical attention. In the United States, people who cannot supply their own basic needs can get help from the government. Citizens have agreed to this by supporting legislation saying that their tax money can be used to help. When tax money is spent in this manner, it is called public welfare. People who receive this money are said to be "on welfare."

What happens to people who cannot support themselves or their families has changed over the years. At one time, people simply did without even the most basic things. In big cities, families lived together in one- or two-room tenement apartments that did not have hot water or bathrooms. Sometimes two families, a total of maybe thirteen or fourteen people, lived in one small apartment. Adults who could not afford rent for an apartment rented floor space. They paid to sleep on the floor in a basement. Those who could not afford even floor space slept in police shelters.

Children ten years old and even younger were thrown out into the street by parents who could not afford to keep

them. They were homeless and had to beg and sleep in doorways. Life was so hard that children were considered lucky if they had jobs working ten or twelve hours a day, six days a week, in a factory. Children, as well as adults, died at alarming rates from lack of proper food and medical care.

Many cities in the United States before and just after the Revolutionary War would make people leave town if they became too poor to do for themselves. In those days most young people were expected to support themselves when they reached the age of fifteen. If they couldn't and their parents refused to provide for them, they would be forced to leave town.

The poorhouse was probably the first form of public welfare in America. Poorhouses were run either by the local government or by private charities. In most cases, people in poorhouses were treated very much like criminals. They were given a place to stay and a small bit of food, and not much more.

The early poorhouses in the United States operated on the belief that the poor were inferior. There is no doubt but that the treatment given the wretched inmates of these institutions was inhumane, but it was seldom criticized. The poor were blamed for their lot. Anything done for

An immigrant to America during the early 1890s. Most immigrants lived in misery. There were few agencies to help them.

them, no matter how small, was thought to be more than they deserved.

In addition to the poorhouses, there were workhouses. These were places where people could get lodging and food in return for work. A man or child might have to work all day breaking rocks with a small hammer for a loaf of bread. Or the food could be a bowl of vegetable soup with a piece of meat in it.

The poor have always been exploited. Most laws regarding child labor were necessary to protect poor children. After all, rich children didn't have to work. But poor children worked twelve or more hours a day in New England mills or in the mines in West Virginia and Kentucky or in New York City's clothing industry. Rich men who wouldn't dream of letting their own children go without schooling or work in dangerous factories would employ the children of the poor at very low wages. Adults too could be forced to work as many hours as an employer wanted because whatever wages they were being paid was better than having no money at all.

Of course, not all people exploited the poor. Many people did as much as they could to relieve the suffering of those less fortunate than themselves. But this kind of help, one person helping another or one family sharing with another, had many limitations. First, there must be

A twelve-year-old boy working in a New York City clothing factory in 1889

someone around with enough to share and with the willingness to share. If there was no surplus or no desire to offer help, a poor person just had to suffer. Second, while a family or an individual might be able to help another for a short time, few people can afford to support another person or a family for very long. So for the most part th poor in America just suffered. Their misery was eased by the limited efforts of charitable individuals and i tions.

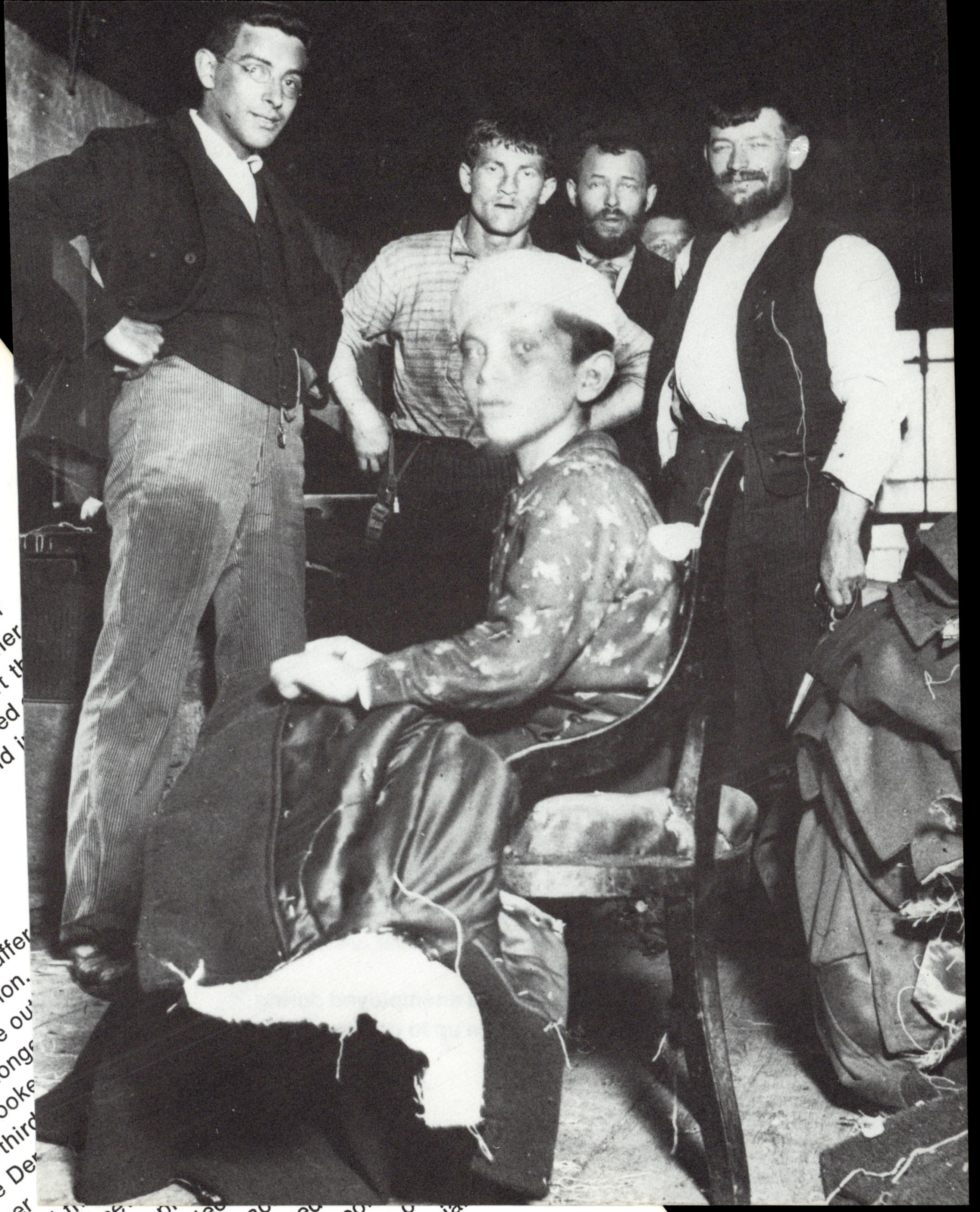

THE DEPRESSION

Beginning in 1929 the United States suffer nomic hardship called a depression. failed and millions of people were ou Depression the poor were no longe They were everywhere you looke jobs available for nearly a third been working before the De President Herbert Hoover His administration believed th just left alone. Franklin D. Roose didate for the Presidency in 1932, p to bring relief to the people. He was ele administration the first national welfare ac The Federal Emergency Relief Act recognized were people who needed the government to suppo Roosevelt's administration was able to institute two major programs to help the needy. They were the Social Security program and unemployment insurance.

Hundreds of peo
the Depressio

A man registering for unemployment insurance

Social Security

The Social Security program is administered directly by the federal government. The government has a percentage of each worker's pay deducted — taken out — and placed in a fund. Then at the age of sixty-five, the worker can retire — stop working — and collect a certain amount of money at regular times, usually once a month. The worker also has a choice of retiring and starting to collect at age sixty-two, but the amount received will be about 20 percent less the whole time he or she is collecting. Also, someone receiving Social Security may work some, earning as much as $2,760 a year, and still receive full Social Security checks. After that, one dollar is deducted for every two dollars earned. The amount a worker gets depends on how much he or she has put into the fund.

In 1973, the Supplementary Security Income (SSI) plan, also a federal program, was begun. This program provides the aged, blind, and disabled who cannot support themselves with whatever additional funds are necessary to bring their income up to a certain minimum amount.

Unemployment Insurance

Persons temporarily out of a job through no fault of their own can collect unemployment insurance. The money comes from a fund into which employers and, usually, employees have put money. Workers in each state do not put in the same amount because each state has its own program. The number of weeks a person can collect unemployment insurance is limited. In most cases, it is less than six months. This is often changed under special conditions.

WHAT IS WELFARE?

Welfare payments differ greatly from either Social Security or unemployment compensation. The most obvious difference is that the person who gets the money has not contributed to a fund. The main requirement for getting welfare is not being able to supply your own basic needs. Although a large part of all the money paid out in Social Security payments is taken from taxes collected from all working people, most Americans think of Social Security payments as "earned" money. The same is true of unemployment compensation. The money paid out to people on welfare also comes directly from taxes, but, because the welfare client has not put money into a welfare fund, these payments are not seen as earned money.

The idea of welfare money not being earned is a sore point for many people. Most Americans believe that there is something good and noble in being able to support themselves and their families. People who cannot support themselves are often looked down upon. During the Depression most of the people who were against the new welfare laws were people who believed in this "work ethic." Even people who worked in the welfare program would make the people who applied for help feel ashamed. Families whose children were too undernourished to go to school were treated as if they were doing something very wrong by asking for help.

By the end of the 1930s, nearly all the general relief programs had been turned over to the states. The states reflected the general negative attitude toward people collecting welfare. States could decide on their own who could collect welfare and who could not. In the South, for example, many blacks were denied welfare even though they needed it, because white welfare workers felt blacks were used to being poor and could stand it better than whites.

ADC — AID TO DEPENDENT CHILDREN

ADC, or Aid to Dependent Children (in some states called AFDC, or Aid to Families with Dependent Children), is and always was one of the most important categories of social welfare. First, let's see how the early program operated.

ADC offered relief to people, usually women, who had children they could not support. ADC also included mothers who could not support their children without leaving them for long periods of time. This program was carried out differently from state to state, from city to city, and even from neighborhood to neighborhood. Women were often subjected to cruel questioning from social workers regarding their morality. A woman who was receiving relief because her husband had deserted her and their children often had to allow her house or apartment to be

Children working as farm laborers
in the South in 1939

searched at odd hours for signs that her husband had returned or that she had some other man there. Many black women were simply denied relief and told to leave their children with relatives or friends while they worked. Many black women accepted jobs as domestics (usually maids in white people's homes) during the day and brought home washing or ironing to do in the evenings. White women were subjected to the same treatment but not as often.

Because of the way the state-administered welfare system was operated, many women who had young children and needed help were rejected. Others simply did not apply.

Today Aid to Dependent Children is the largest social welfare category. To examine the reasons for this, we must first break down the general category into two sections — the **complete family unit** made up of two parents and the **incomplete family unit** with only one parent.

THE COMPLETE FAMILY UNIT

When a complete family unit goes on welfare, it is because the parents cannot make enough money to supply the basic needs of the family. The situation might be that one of the parents becomes ill and cannot work. More likely, the parents no longer can find jobs that will pay enough to cover the family's expenses. Let us take an example.

Mr. and Mrs. Smith have been married for three years. They have two children. Mrs. Smith stays home with the children. Mr. Smith works in a service station. Mr. Smith changes tires, does odd jobs, and sometimes pumps gas. His salary is one hundred and fifty dollars a week. With this he is able to take care of his family. Suddenly, the service station closes because of a lack of business in the neighborhood. Mr. Smith goes to other service stations looking for work, but there are no jobs available.

Mr. Smith then begins to look for other kinds of work. He looks in the help wanted section of the newspaper and applies to local shops. Finally, he finds a job paying one hundred dollars a week. It is the only job he can find, so he takes it. After two weeks he finds that he cannot support his family on that salary.

Mrs. Smith decides to look for a job also. The only job that she can find pays only eighty dollars per week. If she goes to work, it will cost her fifty dollars a week to hire someone to take care of her children and ten dollars a week for carfare. She would have to pay taxes as well. Together, Mr. and Mrs. Smith would not be bringing home as much money as Mr. Smith earned before he lost his job.

Not being able to support his family on his own, Mr. Smith goes to the welfare office and applies for help. If the welfare office finds that he is eligible for assistance, that is, that he makes less than the law says a person needs to support a family the size of his, then Mr. Smith will get supplementary benefits. This means he will get money to add to his salary so that he can provide his family's basic needs.

Every year there are fewer and fewer jobs which an unskilled man such as Mr. Smith can do. To better his con-

The National Guard was called out in Madison, Wisconsin, when mothers camped out to protest cuts in the welfare budget.

dition, Mr. Smith will have to either move his family to a place where there are more unskilled jobs and hope that he can find one that will pay enough to support his family or he must get training so that he can do a skilled job.

Today, many people like Mr. Smith are finding that no matter how hard they are willing to work, they don't have the skills needed for a high-paying job. Years ago, people could almost always find work during times when the country's economy was good. If necessary, they could dig ditches, unload ships, or do other nonskilled labor. Most unskilled jobs are now handled by machines. A machine can dig a ditch in less time than several workers, and more cheaply, too. There is a good possibility that we will eventually reach a point when there will not be enough jobs to keep most people employed. The number of jobs available is an important point to remember when thinking about the reasons people go on welfare.

THE INCOMPLETE FAMILY UNIT

The story of the incomplete family is somewhat different. In the incomplete family, one parent, usually the father, has left the family and no longer helps in its support. Mr. and Mrs. Jones have been married for five years and have three children. Mr. Jones works in a gasoline station, and Mrs. Jones has a part-time job as a school-crossing guard. They don't get along with each other very well, and, after a series of arguments, Mr. Jones moves out of the home and leaves town. Mrs. Jones, who now must care for her three children alone, might very well be forced to apply for welfare.

Other reasons a woman might find herself alone are because her husband dies, or because he commits a crime for which he is sent to prison. But the important point is that the husband is not helping to support his family. Desertion by the father is the most common reason for someone having to go on welfare.

A high percentage of all marriages end with the parents either getting divorced or living apart. But this percentage is higher in poor families that have the added stress of economic hardship. The problem, with regard to welfare, is not that the poor family breaks up but that when it does the husband is not likely to be able to help pay his family's expenses.

The economics of the split-up family are rather easy to see. A man brings home one hundred and forty dollars a week with which to support a family of four (himself, his wife, and two children). He will probably find out that this is barely enough for his family to live on. But he has certain economic advantages. The rent is paid for a house or apartment that is shared by the entire family. Money is spent for food that is also shared by everyone. If the man leaves his family, he has to maintain two households on one paycheck. He must pay his own rent, food, clothes, and utilities, plus his family's, out of his salary of a hundred and forty dollars. Obviously he can't do it.

Another example of an incomplete family is a woman who is not married and has a child whose father is unwilling or unable to help with its support. Often the mother will

have to apply for welfare payments even before the child is born. This happens when her pregnancy makes it impossible for her to work or when she cannot pay the medical bills for prenatal (before birth) care. Both the mother and the child end up on welfare. Being born on welfare is no crime, but it is a great disadvantage, and many welfare children grow up to be welfare parents.

Different people are on welfare for different reasons — your marriage has broken up, or perhaps your skills are not enough to meet the demands of the job market. Perhaps your planning has not been good enough to cope with the situation you find yourself in. An important thing to remember is that people who find themselves on welfare are almost always poor to begin with. Welfare is not usually an easy way out of a sticky situation but rather the last resort of the poor.

WELFARE AND CHEAP LABOR

Labor can become cheap in two ways. One, there are few jobs available and workers must accept what they can get. Two, workers are forced to accept a job no matter how little it pays. In some rural areas, where seasonal workers are needed to pick crops, the checks of welfare clients

Children working as farm laborers in New Jersey in 1970

might be cut during harvesting time. This forces people on welfare to work picking apples or cutting cane or collecting some other crop for low wages. This is not done to encourage people on welfare to work like everybody else. It is done to help the farmer spend less money in wages.

When wages are lowered because of cheap labor, regular workers suffer. For example, you wish to work for Farmer Brown during the harvesting season because you've heard that he pays two dollars an hour. Suddenly Farmer Brown has a supply of people on welfare that he can pay one dollar an hour because their checks have been stopped. You are forced to accept the same salary, despite the fact that you're not collecting welfare.

In places where the welfare system discriminates against minority races, there is very often a situation in which cheap labor is maintained. For instance, if there is a shortage of household workers in an area where blacks do most of the domestic work, a black woman applying for AFDC might not get it. The black woman might be told to leave her children and go to work in someone's house. A white woman, in the same area, might not be expected to leave her children to do housework for someone else. The white woman would get AFDC.

WELFARE AND THE CITIES

The effect of welfare on a city depends on the number of welfare clients compared with the total population. The larger the proportion of welfare clients, the greater the effect on the city.

Let's take a mythical city with a population of 2 million people. We'll call it Center City. Center City's 2 million people are divided into family units of four persons, two adults and two children in each family. This gives us a total of 500,000 families in the entire city. If we decide that in half the families both parents work and in half the families one parent works while the other parent takes care of the children, we then have a total of 750,000 people in Center City who work. If we also decide that it costs the people of Center City $2 million a month to provide the services that the town needs, such as a police department, a fire department, sanitation services, hospitals, schools, a water supply, a license bureau, and so on, then we can see that it would cost each citizen who is working an average of $32 a year in taxes to run the city.

Now let us say that some of the city's population are receiving welfare. This does two things. One, it adds to the cost of running Center City because money is needed to support the people on welfare and to take care of the administrative costs of running a welfare program. If, say, 10,000 families were on welfare, and if we say that it takes $7,000 a year to support a family of four, then it would take 10,000 times $7,000, or $70,000,000 a year, for the support of welfare families. Add $500,000 for administrative costs and the total cost is $70,500,000 a year. Or more than $5.8 million a month.

At the same time, the number of people needing the services of the city has not gone down, so we must add the new costs of welfare to the original $2 million cost of running the city. The monthly bill for running the city is now $7.8 million a month. And where we once had 750,000 people working, we now have 750,000 less the workers in the 10,000 families that are on welfare. Therefore, we now have fewer than 740,000 people to assume the heavy new load. Each person's share of the costs of running the city is now more than $125 a year — almost four times as much as before.

What, then, are the effects on Center City? Well, one is that people who are supporting the city through their tax dollars will be less likely to want to stay in the city. They would rather move into a city where the costs of supporting the city are not so great. Businesses, which also pay local taxes, might also be tempted to move to a location where the taxes are lower. As working people move away from the city, fewer people will be tempted to move into the city. Often the decision to buy a home on the outskirts of a city is made because the expenses of living in the city are the same as those of buying a house.

Well-run day care centers free mothers of young children so that they can get jobs. When such centers are operated at low cost or with no charge to mothers, the money for salaries and supplies usually comes from taxes.

The money to provide free school breakfasts usually comes from taxes.

Some people might be tempted to move into Center City. But they are mostly people who won't help the financial crunch very much. In the small community of Ruralville, where the welfare payments are quite a bit lower, and where people who receive welfare have a difficult time getting by on what they get, the higher welfare payments in Center City could look very attractive. So a family from Ruralville moves to Center City and gets on the welfare rolls there. What does this do to Center City? It makes the burden on Center City, and therefore on the residents of Center City, that much higher. More working people and more businesses that are supplying jobs are tempted to leave. It is clear that if the welfare rolls and taxes do not stop growing, there will soon come a time when people who are working will not want to live in Center City.

Center City can apply to the federal or state government for help, but even this help will not be enough to change the situation very much. The federal and state governments are limited in the amount of money they can offer. In addition, there is a legislative problem. If the state gives money to a particular city or community, that money must come from somewhere. Usually it comes from taxes. The result is that working people in other communities are being taxed to support the welfare clients in Center City. And those people don't like doing it. So, because they don't want to make the voters angry, legislators in other communities will vote against giving money to help Center City. Center City will probably have to raise its own taxes or reduce services to pay for its welfare program.

Without doubt welfare is a financial drain on local governments. The costs to municipal, county, and state funds are enormous. The quality of life in a city can be changed drastically by the costs of its welfare program. Given a limited supply of money, gathered chiefly through tax collection, all sums of money paid out in the way of public assistance must be taken from other programs. Thus, a city with a large welfare program will have to do with decreases in such services as sanitation, police and fire protection, library hours, and so on.

In an urban budget crisis, where a city's money from taxes and state and national sources is not enough to run the city and its programs must be cut back, the one area that is rarely cut is welfare. The reason for this is that cutting relief payments may mean some people would go without basic necessities, while cuts in other areas may result only in inconveniences or slightly greater health and safety risks. Usually, the city leaders decide it is better to keep a museum open for only four days a week than for people to go without food.

A point to remember about welfare, however, is that it is often used to cover up certain problems without really solving them. People on welfare, because they are not begging in the streets or starving, become nearly invisible except to other poor people. When one discusses New York, one talks of skyscrapers, the Statue of Liberty, the great melting pot, and the sophistication of the city. No one mentions that one out of every seven people in the city is receiving some form of welfare.

Someone has to care for the poor in states where welfare is hard to get or where payments are low. Here, a VISTA (Volunteers in Service to America) volunteer brings a free hot lunch to an elderly woman.

Housing designed for the poor and middle class

Many cities across the country are now facing problems similar to those of Center City. It has reached a point where large numbers of people who would normally work and live in the cities are leaving to escape high taxes and poorer services. Businesses, which help support the city, provide jobs, and attract people into the cities, are also leaving. Department stores, for example, are opening branches in suburban areas, following the people who are most likely to spend.

What can Center City do to revive its businesses and attract middle-class people back into the city?

Some cities have started programs where they subsidize (pay part of the cost of) housing for the middle class by lowering the taxes so that building owners may charge less rent. This rarely works, however, because the city's expenses are growing faster than the programs, and expensive services have still been reduced or cut back. As a result, lower apartment rent does not encourage many people to move back to the city.

Center City can try to be more efficient in its administration of the welfare program, but the savings involved in cost-cutting operations are rarely enough to make much of a dent in the overall program.

The most obvious and immediate way to bring middle-class people back to the city is to somehow stop the growing welfare rolls, which are draining the city's resources, so that the city can once again offer the kinds of programs and services that will lure those people back.

NATIONALIZING WELFARE

Many people have advocated nationalizing welfare. They argue that the only way to reduce the burden on certain parts of the country, the cities in particular, is to make welfare payments uniform throughout the country. The rules for getting on welfare would also be the same everywhere. This would mean that it would be just as easy for a person to receive welfare assistance in a small southern town as in a large eastern city.

People who argue against the nationalization of welfare offer several arguments for their point of view. The most common of these arguments is that the large cities that have problems caused by large welfare payments have brought these problems upon themselves. They argue, for example, that New York City has created its own welfare problems by offering larger payments to welfare clients than most other cities. They see nationalization as an aid to larger cities which have created their own problems. They also feel that their own communities will suffer if welfare laws are nationalized because a national law will probably provide lower payments than are now provided by the larger cities. This will mean that people receiving welfare will be attracted to the smaller cities to take advantage of the lower costs of living. Therefore, the people from smaller cities think that nationalizing welfare laws will aid cities that currently have problems but will hurt many smaller communities.

Another argument against nationalizing welfare laws is that it would encourage more people to apply for welfare. A standard law, nationally applied, would probably be a lot less strict than those that now exist in some communities.

What all this boils down to is that the communities that are currently having problems want nationalization and their legislators support proposed laws that would make this a reality. Communities that do not have problems want to avoid nationalization because they feel that it would just bring problems to their communities.

GETTING ON WELFARE

After being married for four years, your husband leaves you without any money in the house or any savings. He has just lost his job as a handyman and cannot send you any money even if he wanted to. None of your friends have money to give you either. You decide to apply to the local department of welfare in your city or town.

The first thing that you will have to do is to fill out an application. If you can't fill it out by yourself, a clerk or social worker will probably help you. On the form, you will have to give such information as name, address, whether you are married or single, whether employed or unemployed, and the names and addresses of your and your husband's nearest relatives. You will also have to give the exact dates of birth of your children, when you were last living with your husband, where he works, where you last worked, and your current expenses. After you have filled out the long questionnaire (thirteen pages in New York City), you will be called in for an interview. During the interview, the social worker attempts to find out several things such as what your immediate needs are. And whether you can get help somewhere else. In many cases, the interview boils down not to whether or not you need relief but whether or not you fulfill federal and local requirements for getting it.

If the department of welfare decides that you are entitled to relief payments, then all the people you have named in your application as close relatives or a marital partner are considered as possible sources of support. They may be interviewed by a social worker to find out if they can give money to you. In some states, your home is visited to see that you actually live where you say you do and if conditions are as you said. You may have to give the department of welfare anything you own that represents money. This might be property or your insurance policy.

Let's say that you are a woman with three children and that you live in New York City. You will be given an amount of money that the Department of Social Services of New York has determined will be enough to fill the needs of you and your children. Your budget will include money for such items as food, rent, utilities (gas and electricity), clothing, and cleaning materials. It will not include money for such items as film for your camera, alcoholic beverages, entertainment, sports equipment, or any other items you may wish to buy but which the Department of Social Services does not feel is essential to your well-being. Of course the family may buy any of these things out of the money provided, but they will not be given additional funds for essentials if they run out of money.

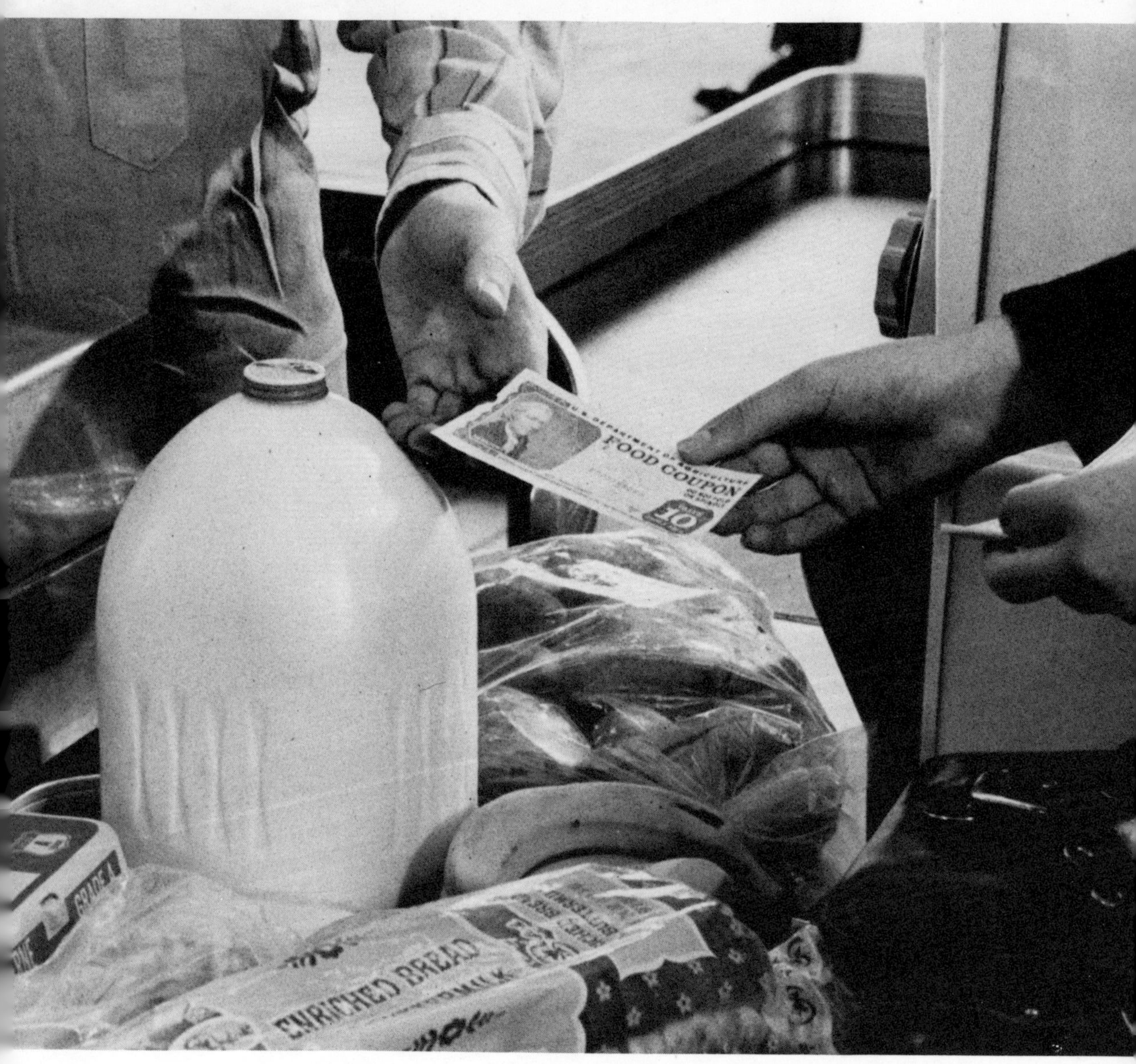

Food stamps

Food Stamps

In addition to your regular payments you will be allowed to purchase a certain amount of food stamps. With food stamps, you can buy food worth more than what you paid for the stamps. Food stamps that cost you eight dollars might allow you to buy ten dollars' worth of food. This means you spend less money to buy groceries.

Housing

The place where you live must also fit the budget requirements of the Department of Social Services. The Department allows a certain amount of money, based on the size of your family, for housing. In many cities and towns, finding decent housing for people on welfare is difficult. Many owners and landlords do not want to rent to welfare clients. Landlords claim welfare people won't take good care of their property because they are not spending their own money for the rent. A more likely reason for not wanting to rent to welfare clients is that people who have made a financial investment in middle-class housing have often made an emotional investment as well. When a person who is very poor moves into a middle-class housing development, the housing loses the value of being a status symbol. And this makes it more difficult to rent the apartment or house to other middle-class people.

Landlords also claim that welfare tenants damage the property more than other people do. There is no real evidence that this is true. Most people want to keep the place they live looking as nice as possible. What often happens is just the opposite. Landlords neglect the buildings where welfare tenants live.

Most Americans agree that people should, at least, live in safe housing.

Many Americans think this kind of housing is too good for the poor.

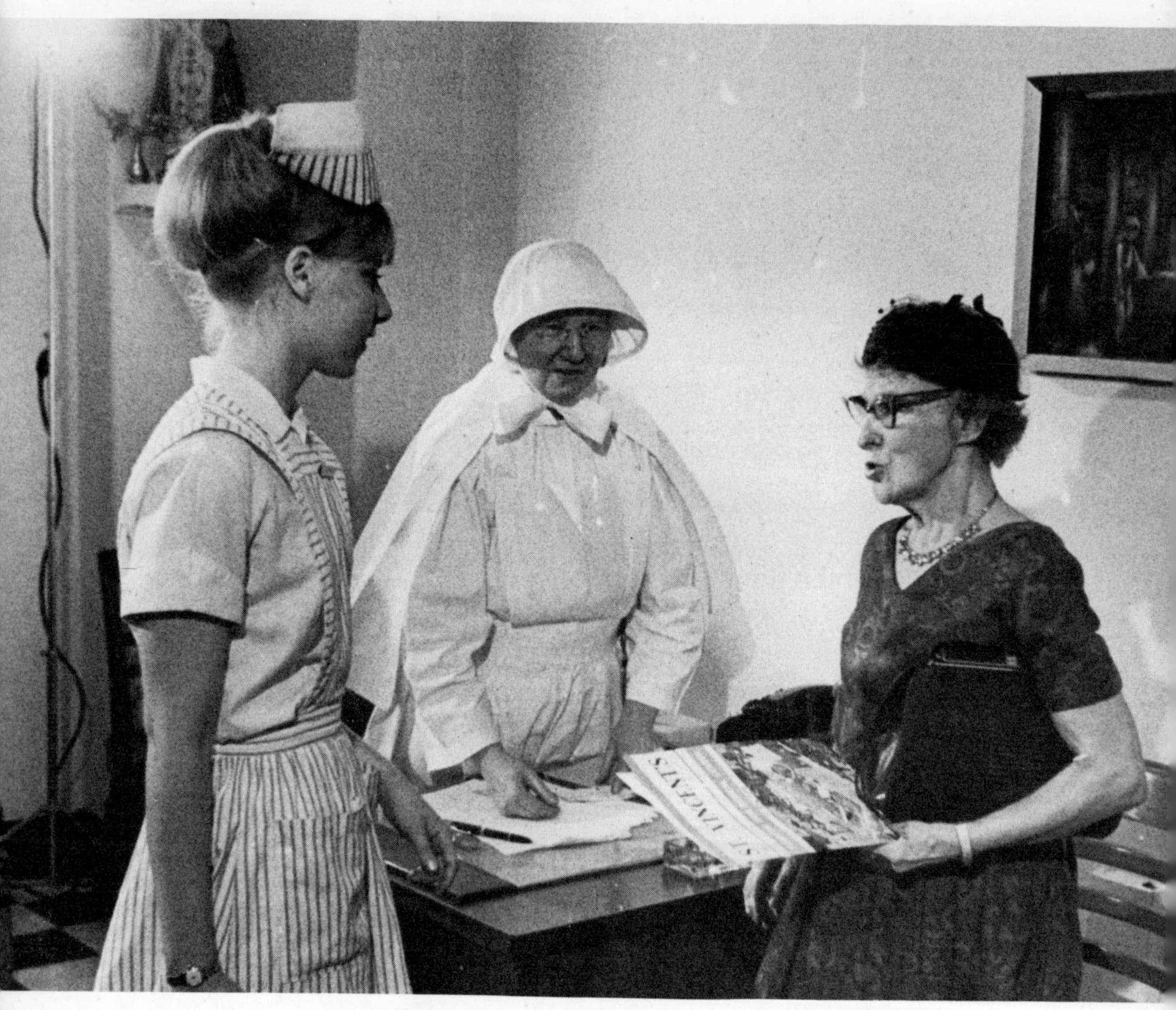

A woman being admitted to a hospital. Low-cost or free medical care is available to the elderly and the poor through the Medicare and Medicaid programs.

When a family who is receiving welfare wishes to move to a better apartment or house, they must apply to the welfare agency for permission and money to move. Usually, the welfare agency must be convinced *not* that the new home is more desirable but that it is impossible for the family to live in health and safety in the old home. Therefore, no matter how unhappy a family is in their present home, they will probably not be given money to move so long as the housing lives up to the minimal standards of the welfare agency.

Medical Needs

Usually your medical needs will be taken care of by the welfare agency. Normally you are given an identification card which indicates that your medical expenses will be paid under the medicaid program. This is a national program available to people who otherwise cannot afford medical care. You do not have to be on welfare to receive medicaid. Doctors and hospitals that treat you or give you medicines bill the welfare agency, which, in turn, is partially repaid by the federal government. Drug stores often accept this billing system as well.

Although the payment of the medicaid patient's bills is guaranteed by the federal government, many hospitals and doctors do not accept patients under this program. Hospitals run by the city, municipality, or other local form of government usually do accept medicaid. Although the United States is among the world's leaders in health care, the care given to the very poor still does not compare favorably with that given to the middle and upper classes. Still, people on welfare do not have to worry about basic health care.

GETTING OFF WELFARE

Most of us live considerably better than people on welfare do. The problems associated with being on welfare — poor housing, never having enough money to do the things you want, having to depend on an impersonal agency for all of your needs — are more than enough reasons for wanting to get off welfare. But to give a person the incentive to try to get off welfare you must make being off welfare more attractive than being on.

Obviously, if people's lives are going to become worse when they stop receiving checks, they will want to stay on welfare. So to get people back into the labor force so that they can earn their own living, they must be offered more than they are receiving from the welfare agency. This additional offering might be in the form of more money, pride, a sense of self-reliance, or escape from the tight regulation of the welfare agency. In no case, can the quality of life go down.

A welfare mother with eight children, living in New York, for example, receives approximately $371 twice a month, or $742 a month. From this she has to cover all her family's needs. A typical monthly budget might be:

Rent (for four-bedroom apartment)	$300.00
Food ($199 of this in form of food stamps)	300.00
Utilities and phone	50.00
Clothing	40.00
Miscellaneous (non-food supermarket items)	52.00
	$742.00

Meeting the moderate basic expenses requires $8,904 a year. This amount is $13 more than the average working family earns each year after taxes and other deductions. This welfare mother's budget does not include items that go with having a job such as carfare, additional clothing, and, because of the age of the children, a baby-sitter. Adding these items to the budget we get:

Carfare (20 days @ $1 a day)	$ 20.00
Clothing (cleaning and upkeep)	20.00
Child care ($12 a day for 22 days)	264.00
	$304.00

The budget is increased by $304 per month, bringing the total monthly expenses to $1,046, or $12,552 a year, as the *net* (after taxes and other deductions) budget necessary just to provide the family's basic needs. To earn this amount on a job, the welfare mother would need a salary of more than $250 per week. The possibility of the average welfare client making $250 per week, $108 more than the national average salary, is remote. If this particular family had but one desire — to get off welfare — it would be practically impossible.

Of course, smaller earnings would be enough to support a family with fewer children. Even so, a woman with two children who gets seventy dollars a week from welfare is not likely to net this amount after child care, carfare, and withholding taxes on a job.

The threat of not being able to earn enough money is one risk of getting off welfare. Under our present system, people receiving public assistance cannot earn the same amount of money that the welfare agency has decided is a minimum figure for their health, safety, and well-being. Retraining is one method welfare agencies are using to help clients get better jobs.

Retraining

Training programs teach people to do work such as typing, clerical tasks, hospital jobs, and many other kinds of labor. The programs also teach basic academic skills. Few people, however, get off welfare simply by being retrained. There are three basic reasons for this. The first is that most people on welfare are either children or women taking care of small children. If training is to help these women, they must be trained for jobs that are going to pay enough to support themselves and their children plus pay for babysitting services. Most courses currently available in retraining programs do not lead to jobs that pay enough to cover all these expenses.

Second, few welfare clients have the educational background necessary to be trained for high-paying jobs. Computer programming, for example, might pay enough for a woman with two children (the average family on

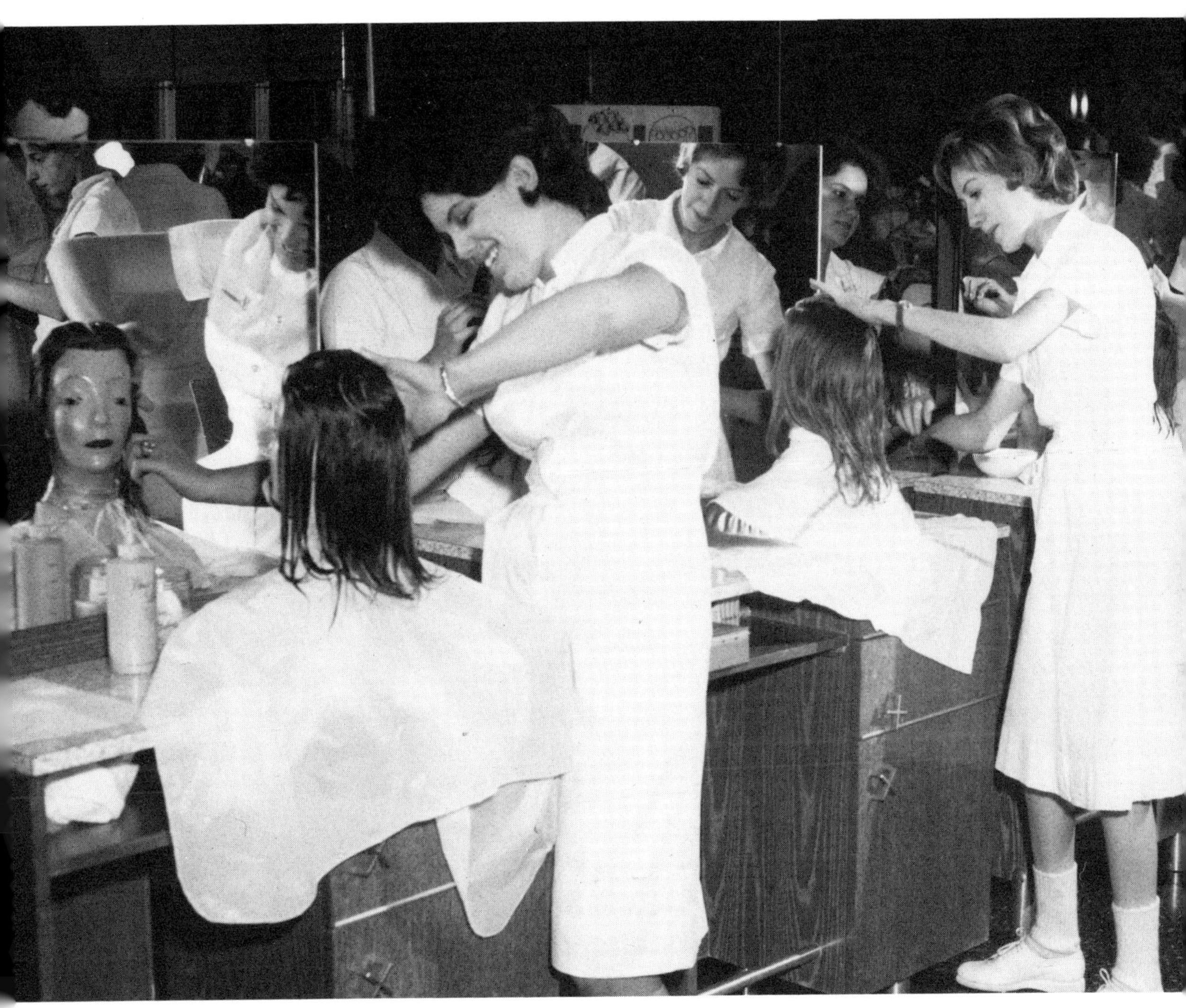

The beauty field is one area where retraining can result in getting a steady job.

AFDC has 3.4 members) to get off welfare, but the welfare client will probably not have the academic skills needed to pass the course. In fact, few Americans, on welfare or not, have good enough academic skills to complete this kind of training.

The third reason retraining doesn't get most people off welfare is the cost of the training. The cost of really meaningful training, which in most cases would include academic training as well as occupational training, would be greater than the cost of any welfare program we've discussed so far.

Talking with a Welfare Mother

"I used to live in South Carolina and sometimes I would travel back and forth to New York and do domestic work. Mostly sleep-in jobs." Mrs. M. is a large black woman. Her apartment is clean and neatly furnished. Wanda, her four-year-old daughter, sits at the far end of the couch trying to attract her mother's attention without actually interrupting her. "After me and my husband broke up I applied for help in South Carolina, but they said I didn't need help, which was a lie. So the next time I came to New York I decided to stay. My husband came to New York, too, and we got back together again. The kids were still in South Carolina. He got sick right after that, and depressed, and we split up again.

"When I was living in South Carolina, my mother used to help me take care of the children, but she was getting old and everything, and she could hardly do for herself, let alone help me out.

"So at first I was sending money down to her from my sleep-in jobs, but after a while she wrote to me and said that I would have to come down and help take care of the kids. It wasn't any use for me to go down there because if I did and had to care for the kids I couldn't make any money. So I went down and got them and brought them to New York. I had a friend who kept them for me during the week while I worked, but that didn't last too long. That's when I first applied to the welfare department.

"I don't know, maybe I wouldn't have had as many children [Mrs. M. has ten children — eight of them are at home] if I knew I was going to be on welfare. But I thought things were going to be okay, that they would work themselves out. You know, people have children and they take care of them. It ain't having children what's so bad, it's not having the money to take care of them proper."

I repeated to Mrs. M. the theory I had often heard that the more children a welfare mother gets the more money she gets and the easier she has it. She crossed her arms over her chest and leaned back in her chair. Her lips were tight as she spoke.

"You know what my budget is? I get $371 twice a month. Out of that I got to pay $230 a month for rent, between $40 and $50 a month for gas and electricity, and $198 for food stamps. Those food stamps don't count toward things like toilet tissue, soap, and that kind of stuff. I can't even buy toothpaste with them food stamps. Anyway,

I spend at least ten extra dollars a week at the supermarket on cleaning stuff and toothpaste and things. If one of the children wants a handkerchief or needs a pair of shoes, then I got to take it from that money. If they want five cents to buy a piece of chocolate, I got to take it out of that budget. If my boy needs a suit dry-cleaned, that comes out of that budget. I sit up here broke so many days I don't know what to do with myself.

"Not only that, but when you have a young baby or two young babies you're chained to the house. Some mothers will go out and leave their children, but most won't. You don't even get a chance to go to a movie unless you can find somebody who'll baby-sit for you. And half the time you don't have the money to go to a movie, anyway. I'd like to be able to go out and do something, sometimes. You know, to be useful to somebody. Living on a welfare budget is like the worse thing a woman can do to herself. When you don't have a man coming home in the evening, it's even worse, because all day is like ten o'clock in the morning.

"I'd love to get off welfare. I've never been the kind of person who'd just sit home and collect checks on the first and sixteenth. It used to be the third and the eighteenth. I've always been one to get out and get some kind of job. Mostly I did domestic work. Since I been on welfare I've had some training. I was trained as a keypunch operator down on Rivington Street. I don't think anybody that got that kind of training class in keypunch ever got a regular job out of it. The kind of training they want to give you don't really add up to much. What you really need is something that will guarantee you a job instead of all that window-dressing training they give you. I don't know anyone who ever got a job from the welfare department except the people who work in the welfare department. They have a whole welfare industry in New York.

"Life ain't what you would call terrible, you know. What I mean is that I can see where I'd be a lot worse off in other circumstances, you see. But it's no way to live. Not for anyone who wants to do more than get up in the morning and go to bed at night. It's just no way to live."

Two of Mrs. M.'s ten children are out on their own. Her oldest boy is currently serving in the armed forces, and her oldest daughter has children and a welfare budget of her own.

ALTERNATIVES TO WELFARE

Income Redistribution

The relationship between what poor people earn and what not-poor people earn is more important than the actual amount that either of them earns. If you were making two hundred dollars a week and everybody else was making two hundred dollars a week you would be as well off as most people. If everybody else was only making fifty dollars a week you would be a lot better off than most people. On the other hand, if you were making two hundred dollars a week and everybody else was making a thousand dollars a week, you would be poor and might have to apply for welfare.

It might be possible to reduce the number of people on welfare if we could narrow the gap between poor people and not-poor people. This is called income redistribution. And several plans have been suggested.

Negative Income Tax

Under the negative income tax plan, people making less than a certain amount, let's say four thousand dollars, would not have to pay income taxes, and they would be given enough money to bring their earnings up to four thousand dollars. A family making three thousand dollars, for example, would be given a thousand dollars to bring their income for the year up to four thousand.

There are several problems with this plan. The first problem is simply how to carry it out. If, for example, a family's income is less than the minimum for its size throughout the year, how will it support itself while waiting for its yearly earnings to be determined so that it can receive additional funds? If a family makes two hundred dollars a month for six months, should it be assumed that it will make only two hundred dollars for the next six months and be given the money to bring it up to the four thousand dollar level? What if the family then makes more than four thousand dollars? Again, if the money is given as a lump sum, is it as effective as providing a regular income on a monthly basis? Probably not.

A second practical problem is how to decide on the minimum income figures — how much a family really needs to get along. Would a rural family require as much to live on as an urban family? Can we realistically expect states with few poverty problems to vote for as high a minimum as states with a large problem? After all, the tax money of the states with less of a problem would end up flowing over to support poor people in other states. The program of negative income tax seems to be much too cumbersome to effectively replace the present system of direct cash grants.

Guaranteed Annual Income

This is essentially the same program as the negative income tax and has the same problems. One of the main problems with this or any plan that guarantees a minimum income is that of job overlap. Let's say two families, each made up of two parents and four children, each need fifteen thousand dollars a year to live on. In family A, both parents work and together they earn fifteen thousand dollars. In family B, only the father works, and he makes seven thousand dollars a year. His family is then given the additional eight thousand by the government. Why then should both parents in family A work, when they can get the same as family B even if one parent stays home?

A third family, family C, is made up of a woman and five children. They too need fifteen thousand dollars a year. No one in this family works and the government supplies the entire amount. Since it costs more to work than it does to stay home (carfare, lunches, dry cleaning bills, baby-sitters), the family that does the least work will have the greatest benefits. For this reason, the guaranteed annual income plan is said to discourage people from working.

Asset Taxation

This plan proposes to tax all assets — valuables, such as property, as well as income — on a strictly progressive scale. In other words, the more you have, the more taxes you pay.

A house, for example, is an asset. A person who buys a house or business property is now allowed to deduct the interest and taxes he pays for the house or property from his taxable income. John buys a house for forty thousand dollars. His monthly payment, including taxes and interest, is three hundred and fifty dollars per month. Out of this amount, two hundred dollars per month is either tax payments or interest on the mortgage. John is allowed to deduct the two hundred dollars per month, or twenty-four hundred dollars per year, from his taxable income.

Joe, on the other hand, rents an apartment. He does not own it so it is not an asset. His rent is three hundred dollars per month. But since Joe is not paying interest on a mortgage or taxes on the property he is not allowed to deduct any of the cost of the apartment rental. The present tax system is obviously a disadvantage to Joe and an advantage to John.

Under our present tax system, income is taxed in a more or less progressive manner. A person making three thousand dollars might be taxed at 10 percent; a person making twelve thousand, at 18 percent; a person making sixty thousand, at 55 percent. In theory this seems to be progressive taxation, but in fact it isn't. The reason is that the higher your income the more likely you are to have earnings from nonprogressively taxed sources. A person who makes money in the stock market is often taxed less for these earnings than for other income. A person making ten thousand dollars in the stock market will pay much less tax on it than another person making a salary of ten thousand dollars.

For example, both Joe and John make ten thousand dollars a year. But John makes his money from dividends in the stock market. The dividend is John's share of the profits of the company whose stock he owns. Joe makes his ten thousand as salary. Under the present tax system, Joe might end up paying five to ten times more in taxes than John who is a much wealthier man!

The disadvantages of the asset taxation program are less obvious than those of the negative income tax. John is given tax breaks to encourage him and people like him to invest their money in ways that will help the economy of the entire country. If no one invested money in the stock market, for example, many businesses would have to stop their operations and many jobs would be lost. However, the result of investors paying lower taxes is that people with more money are allowed to widen the gap between themselves and people with less money. It costs more to be poor than it does to be rich.

Food and Housing Subsidies

This is a program in which food and housing would be subsidized by the government. All families with an annual income below twenty thousand dollars would be given stamps for food and housing according to family size. The food stamp program is a step in this direction. Under the food and housing subsidy program, people with the least money are helped more than people with a higher income. A family of four earning ten thousand dollars a year is subsidized four thousand dollars, an increase of 40 percent.

A family of four making only four thousand dollars would have an increase of 100 percent. But the drawbacks to this program, as is the case with many programs, is the cost. Any program designed to ease economic problems in one area must be weighed against possible problems in other areas. The costs of across-the-board food or rent subsidies which would better distribute the country's wealth would cost so much in additional taxes that the population of the state or the federal government could never afford it.

Social Welfare Insurance

Social welfare insurance is a plan whereby people who are working would be taxed as they are for unemployment insurance. The money would go into a fund which would be used by people needing welfare. What this would do is remove the stigma from receiving welfare. It would not be a true "insurance," since the people who put the most into such a fund would be those least likely to need to draw upon it. Also, inasmuch as a majority of welfare clients are children who will not be putting any money into the fund, the idea of calling it insurance becomes meaningless.

THE FUTURE OF WELFARE

When considering the future of welfare one must first look at its past. The first welfare programs in this country began during the Depression. Their purpose was to offer emergency help to those who needed it. When public welfare was turned over to the states, problems developed and began to multiply. One of the major causes of the problems was that welfare administrators had different opinions about the purpose of welfare. The attitudes varied from state to state and even within the same office, as welfare workers brought their own beliefs into the system. Some saw it only as a form of emergency aid, others saw it as a way of helping people maintain a decent standard of living, and still others saw it as a haven for lazy people who didn't want to work. Changes in welfare laws have been slow in coming. Although there is now far greater dignity in applying for and being on welfare, a certain amount of disgrace still remains.

In good economic times, few people complain about welfare costs. In bad economic times, there are many complaints. At the time this book is being written, welfare costs have been the object of bitter complaints in many urban communities. The staggering costs of welfare have hurt the cities. In addition, cities with high welfare populations have been faced with businesses moving out because of high taxes, and with neighborhoods crumbling because the people who live in them don't have money to keep them up.

There is no indication that welfare rolls will decrease. If the trend of the sixties and seventies shows anything, it is that there will probably be even more people on welfare in the future. One of the reasons for this is that machines are replacing unskilled workers. Years ago, it took several men hours to dig a ditch that one man using a machine can now do in minutes. Although this frees people to do other kinds of work, it is only good if there are other kinds of work to do.

Throughout history, circumstances have forced some women to be the sole supporters of their children. In the past, uneducated women could take unskilled jobs and make out. Today few unskilled jobs pay enough and the cost of living is so high that not many women alone with children can be self-supporting. More than likely, the same woman who could have worked and supported herself years ago will be forced onto the welfare rolls today.

As a boy, the author lived in a building in which only blue-collar workers lived. These people worked in factories or at shipyards, drove trucks, or did similar kinds of work. Most of the work took little skill and depended on strength or physical activity. Now, many jobs in this area do not exist. People who worked on these jobs in years past can no longer find them and are forced onto welfare.

Hundreds of people line up outside a welfare office to get their checks. Sadly, throughout America, the lines are getting longer.

Since its beginning during the Depression, public welfare has meant different things to different people. To some, it has been a needless giveaway by the government to those who are not willing to work for a living. To others, it has been a humanitarian act to relieve suffering. To still others, it has been the support of immoral people whose bad habits have caused their own miseries.

But to millions of people who are receiving public assistance, it has been a way to survive with less suffering than they would have had to endure if there were no welfare.

The public welfare program in the United States today is far from perfect. As the country changes, both socially and economically, changes are needed in the welfare system too. Methods of taxing people to pay for the program will have to be changed so that certain segments of the country will not have to pay more than others for what is obviously a national problem. Much more will have to be done to make sure that the national wealth is spread out more evenly to reduce the number of people who suffer because they are poor.

SOME QUESTIONS ABOUT WELFARE

1. If at one time there was no welfare, or public assistance programs, in the United States and people survived, why not just cut out all present programs? Won't people still survive?

A. Yes, people will, for the most part, survive. But as a society we must decide where we are to place our values. Although in the past when there were no public assistance programs people did survive, they did so only with great suffering and hardship. The number of babies who died at birth was extremely high, and the quality of life for the poor was extremely low. Children often roamed the street, sick and homeless, because their parents couldn't support them. Entire families often lived in small, airless tenements in a state of abject misery. Do we really want these conditions, or even worse, again?

2. The largest increase in welfare costs since 1964 has been in the AFDC program, that is, for people who have babies that they either can't or won't support. Why should I have to contribute to their support?

A. The main reason, of course, is that you have no choice. In a democracy the minority has to go along with the decisions of the majority. In this case, the majority of Americans have decided that it is better to provide for these children than to allow them to go without the basic necessities: food, shelter, and clothing. People who do not want to provide for these children must convince the majority of Americans to go along with their point of view. If this can be done, the society will no longer provide for children whose parents cannot afford to take care of them.

3. Why doesn't the national government take over the public assistance programs to relieve the burdens on the cities?

A. Because for the Federal government to pass a law nationalizing public assistance, both the Senate and the House would have to vote for such a law. But congressmen whose districts don't have large welfare populations will not benefit from such legislation; neither will the voters they represent. Congressmen and voters who will not be helped by such a law will defeat it. Only those people who would benefit most directly, people in large urban areas, would probably support such a bill to nationalize welfare.

4. Can't we just limit the number of people in any city who can receive welfare payments?

A. Yes, we can do this, but what would be accomplished? Some cities once prohibited the poor from settling in their areas, but this only caused the poor to move on to some city where they were allowed to live. The same would probably be true of welfare. People who need it would just have to move to another city.

5. How about giving women who apply for AFDC a choice of being sterilized or not getting public assistance?

A. This could only be done if the majority of Americans decided it was desirable and began the long legal process of trying to get such a decision passed into a law that would not be declared unconstitutional by the Supreme Court or struck down by actions of Congress.

6. Granted, we don't want to create a source of cheap private labor, but why can't we make some of the welfare recipients work on public projects such as keeping the parks clean, cleaning graffiti from public buildings, and things like that? Then they would be contributing to the same people who contribute to them.

A. There have been programs designed to do just this. One of them is the Work Relief Employment Program in New York City, and another is the Comprehensive Employment Training Act, which is a federal program. The problems with both these programs is that they are often little more than "make work" projects and do not really prepare welfare clients to compete for jobs under normal conditions. The programs also compete with existing jobs, such as street cleaners and park department workers. In addition, many of them are part time and demand little from the worker, so they don't prepare the worker to hold a regular job even if he or she gets one.

7. Darwin said that civilization advances by the survival of the fittest. Wouldn't our society actually benefit if the able-bodied people in our society did not tie themselves to those who are not able-bodied?

A. What Darwin really said was that in the natural order of things those creatures who best fit their environment are most likely to survive. Civilized man, however, is attempting to create his own order. And if we're talking about natural orders and survival of the fittest, would you mind it if people on welfare took your possessions by force? That would be natural order as well. Our society is not built on the premise of natural order, but has been molded in a way that we feel has benefit to the largest number of people and which allows us to live with the social and moral standards we desire.

8. Speaking of moral standards, aren't we rewarding immorality when we support a woman who has a child and is not married?

A. We are supporting the child, who is neither moral nor immoral, and we support the mother so that she can care for the child.

9. Does welfare change people?

A. Welfare itself does not change people, because it

is basically just a means of survival. The fact that it is almost impossible for people to get off welfare perhaps changes people because they cannot have dreams of a better future.

10. How much do the welfare benefits vary from one state to another?

A. The differences in some cases are quite large. Mississippi, for example, pays an average that is only one-fifth of the average paid in New York. The highest-paying states are Massachusetts, Connecticut, New York, and Hawaii.

11. Is the purpose of welfare to support people or to help them over temporary difficulties?

A. Although individual programs have been defined and redefined, there is no nationally accepted definition of the purpose of welfare. Some people claim that the purpose of welfare is simply not to allow people to suffer unduly in a rich society. But people are often allowed to suffer, anyway. Those who claim that the welfare program is only temporary help for the clients must face the fact that little money is spent to help people get off welfare.

12. Isn't it true that most people on welfare are black?

A. No. There are more whites on welfare in the United States than blacks. But the more important fact to consider is that the percentage of blacks on welfare is extremely high. Blacks make up about 45 percent of the total welfare population, but only 12 percent of the national population. According to government figures, one out of every four blacks in the United States is receiving some form of public welfare.

13. Will our welfare population decrease over the next ten years?

A. The number of people needing welfare assistance will probably not decrease if present trends continue. These trends are (1) a decrease in the total amount of available jobs per worker, (2) a decrease in the number of stable family units, and (3) an increase in the flow of wealth to the already well-to-do people. These facts all mean the welfare rolls will probably continue growing over the next ten years.

INDEX

ABOUT THE AUTHOR

Walter Dean Myers is the author of many juvenile books, including *The Dancers, The World of Work,* and *Fast Sam, Cool Clyde and Stuff.* He has written articles and stories for *Essence, Scholastic Magazine,* and *McCall's.* In 1968 he won the award for the best juvenile manuscript of the year from the Council on Interracial Books for Children for his book *Where Does the Day Go?* Mr. Myers is at present employed as a book editor with a major New York City publishing company.